CYRIL DAVEY

MOTHER TERESA

Missionary to the Poor

Hunt & Thorpe

Copyright © 1992 Hunt & Thorpe
Text © 1992 by Cyril Davey
Originally published by Hunt & Thorpe 1992
ISBN 1 85608 012 9

In Australia this book is published by:
Hunt & Thorpe Australia Pty Ltd.
9 Euston Street, Rydalmere NSW 2116

Acknowledgments
Camera Press: cover, 13, 24, 27 right, 31.
Church Missionary Society: 8/9, 14, 20/21.
LEPRA: 40, 41.
Gillian Payne: 40.
Popperfoto: 6, 13, 20, 21, 24 left, 25, 47.
Simon Weinstock: 5, 29, 32/33, 36/37, 44/45.
Illustrations. Deborah Noble: 16/17, 19, 23, 34.

A CIP catalogue record for this book is available from the British Library.

Manufactured in U.K.

CONTENTS

1

"SOMEBODY SHOULD DO SOMETHING"

The slim, short woman in the white sari made her way carefully along the street on the crowded pavement. Thin children begged in the gutters; bony cows dragged heavy carts along the street; families, living on the wide pavement, squatted near tiny fires trying to cook a small meal of rice and curry. This was over-crowded, poverty-stricken Calcutta, India, one of the biggest cities of the world.

The woman bent down over something huddled against the wall. She was a white woman, dressed as an Indian, and there was a small silver cross by her shoulder. No Hindu woman would wear *that*! The wall was the outside wall of a hospital, and what lay there was all that remained of a man, thin as a skeleton. The woman went swiftly into the hospital, but was as quickly turned away. They could do nothing for people like that ... there were hundreds of them in Calcutta ... refugees, many of them. "He will die anyway! Medicine would be no good!" they told her.

And indeed, when she went back and bent over him the man *was* dead. He had died while she was trying to get the hospital to help.

"Somebody *must* do something!" she said. Her name was Mother Teresa, a Roman Catholic nun who had already lived in India for more than twenty years. And, sent by God, she *did* do something.

This book tells the story of who she is and what she did.

2
AGNES

She was really named Agnes Bojaxhiu—her other name, Teresa, was given to her when she became a nun—and she was born in 1910 in Skopje, a small town in Yugoslavia, the country lying between Italy and Greece, in the Mediterranean Sea. Her sister, Aga, and Lazar, their brother, were both older than Agnes, but they were a very close family where the children played together, walked, talked, and sang songs together, as country families do. Because they were a devout family they went to church together, too, and Drana, their mother, tried to make sure that Jesus was very real to them.

Their father, Kole, was a merchant who traveled a great deal in other countries, and when he came home from Turkey or Egypt or Greece he had strange-looking presents for them and wonderful stories to tell. He was surely the best dad in the world! And then, when Agnes was eight, he came home from a long journey looking very ill. He was rushed off to the hospital at once, but a few days later he died.

Now there would be no more stories, no more presents ... and it would be Drana, their mother, who had to support the family. There would be less money for clothes and food ... less money for the poor people Kole and Drana had always helped, the children thought.

But that was one thing that did not change.

Beggars in a Calcutta street.

7

3

"POOR PEOPLE ARE SPECIAL PEOPLE"

Agnes was still sent to take some dinner to the old widow down the road, when her mother could not go. Often someone who dropped in would be asked to share a meal already cooking in the pot, and that meant less for the children. "Never eat food," Drana would say to them, "unless you are prepared to share it with someone who has none!"

There seemed to be more people in the house now than when their father Kole was alive, and Drana seldom had time to sit down, so it seemed. And yet she always had time for prayer at home, and worship in church, not every *week* but every *day*. As she grew older, Agnes came to feel that her mother loved people as much as she loved God. One day she asked Drana why she did so much for very ordinary, very poor people who could give her nothing in return.

"Poor people," said her mother, "are God's *special* people. God expects us to serve them as we would serve Jesus if he were here."

It would be a very long time before Agnes came to feel that the poor people of India were, for her, the most special of all. Indeed, as she came to her twelfth birthday, Agnes had not begun to think about India at all; but she *did* know what she *wanted* to do. She wanted to be a teacher—and everyone was sure she would make a very good one.

Indian landscape. The Nilgiri Hills, with tea plantations.

4

AGNES MAKES UP HER MIND

Yes, she would certainly make a very good teacher indeed, her mother agreed. But, though she did not say so, she was beginning to feel that Agnes was not going to teach in her own country. She had something else in her heart, too.

She was a quiet girl; clever at school; nice-looking, with bright, dark eyes; never bossy but always a leader in youth activities in her church. She enjoyed music and drama, outings and games, but she was certainly happiest when she was doing some activity connected with the church. She never found the worship dull, the sermons boring, or the prayers too long. God was very real to her when she reached her teens, and she thought he might want her for something special.

Their young priest was especially interested in missions, and Agnes caught his enthusiasm and read everything she could find about the Yugoslavian missionaries in North India. Then, when she was about seventeen, she shared with her family what she thought God wanted her to do.

"I do want to be a teacher, yes ... but I want to belong *completely* to God ... never to get married or anything like that ... just to be God's servant and do what he wants wherever he wants me to be."

Her brother, Lazar, was shocked. "You mean—be a nun? What a waste! All your talents and you want to shut yourself up in a convent!"

"But it won't be like that," said Agnes. "Yes, I *do* want to be a nun ... *and* a teacher ... but I think God wants me to be a missionary, too ... in India!"

5
AGNES BECOMES "TERESA"

It seemed as if all the people she knew in Skopje were at the railway station—grandmothers and little children, priests and schoolteachers and all her teenage friends ... singing, crying, hugging, waving to the quiet eighteen-year-old girl as she got into the train. Agnes herself stood by the window, waving back until the station was out of sight. She was not yet going to India but, with another Yugoslavian girl, she was going to Ireland, to the convent of the Loretto Sisters in Dublin. There she would begin her training as a nun, being dedicated to God and to the service of other people. In these months in Dublin, too, she would have to learn English—the language spoken by all educated Indians.

They spent two months in Dublin before setting sail for India, and in that time there was one quite special happening that showed they had made a new beginning in life. They gave up their "real" names and took "religious" ones.

Agnes Bojaxhiu (which was how her own family would always know her) became 'Sister Teresa'—and Teresa she would be to the end of her life.

Their sea voyage ended in Madras and they spent a day or so there before going on by train to Calcutta. From the ship the country had looked beautiful, with thatched huts and palm trees, but Madras was a big city, hot, noisy, and very full of people. They chattered, shouted, and argued at the tops of their voices, and she realised that they were poorer than any people she had ever seen. Were *all* Indians like this? Agnes-Teresa wondered.

6
IN THE HILLS

Darjeeling is an Indian hill town in beautiful country, with magnificent views of the snow-clad Himalayas, including Mt. Everest itself. It was here that she was sent, first of all, to the main house of the Loretto Sisters to which she now belonged. There were splendid boarding schools for Indian and European children, and Teresa was to teach in the convent school. She thanked God every day in her prayers for his goodness—she was a teacher and a missionary and she belonged completely to God.

But Darjeeling and the district around it were not all as lovely as they seemed. Part of Teresa's time was spent in a small hospital run by the nursing sisters from the convent. Every morning, as soon as the door was opened, she found the veranda crowded with hill people who had often walked hours to get there. Their feet or bodies or faces were disfigured by sores; some coughed terribly with chest complaints; a few had twisted hands or feet, and she learned that these were signs of leprosy. Some were blind. Mothers thrust babies at her, shouting in languages she could not understand.

On the wall of the dispensary there was a colored picture of Jesus, surrounded by sick men, women, and children—and Teresa had a wonderful feeling that she was actually sharing in the healing work of Jesus.

Then, suddenly, it came to an end—the lovely hills, the neat schoolchildren, the crowds of sick hill people. Nineteen-year-old Sister Teresa was moved to Calcutta, and there she would spend the rest of her life.

· F · A · C · T · S · H · E · E · T ·

DATES

1910 August 29	Agnes Gonxha Bojaxhiu born at Skopje, Yugoslavia	
1928 November	Went to Loretto convent, Dublin, to begin her training as a nun. Took the name "Sister Teresa"	Age 18
1929 January	Teaching at St. Mary's school, at Loretto convent,	Age 18–38
1948 August	Entally, Calcutta (Headmistress from 1937)	
1946 September 10	"Inspiration Day" when Mother Teresa heard God's call to serve the poor	Age 35
1948	Mother Teresa became an Indian citizen	
1948 January	Asked permission to live outside the convent	Age 37
1948 August 18	Laid aside her nun's habit and put on an Indian woman's sari. Left the convent and went to the American Missionary Sisters' hospital at Patna for three months. Returned to live with the Little Sisters of the Poor just before Christmas.	Age 37
1948 December 21	Opened her first school in Moti Jheel	Age 38
1949 February	Moved into Michael Gomes's house	Age 38
1949 March 19	Joined by her first recruit, Subhasini Das	Age 38
1950 October 7	New Congregation of Missionaries of Charity approved by Rome	Age 39
	Mother House founded at 54a Lower Circular Road, Calcutta	
1963 March 25	Archbishop of Calcutta blessed the beginnings of the Missionary Brothers of Charity	Age 52
1965 July	Mother Teresa went to Caracas, Venezuela, to open the first Center outside India	Age 54
1977	Sisters of the Word, a contemplative branch of Missionaries of Charity, founded in New York	Age 66
1977 June	Received honorary degree of Doctor of Divinity at Cambridge University, from Prince Charles	
1978	Brothers of the Word founded in Rome	Age 67
1978 July	Received The Order of the British Empire from the Australian High Commissioner, in Delhi	
1979	Awarded the Nobel Peace Prize	Age 68
1983	Over two hundred Houses of Missionaries of Charity had been founded in fifty-two countries	Age 72
1983 November	Order of Merit presented by the Queen of England in India	
1984	Missionaries of Charity Fathers founded	Age 73

p) In action in Calcutta.
low) Pope John Paul II visits
ther Teresa. (Right) Sisters of the
:sionaries of Charity, reading the
·le.

7
SCHOOLS FOR RICH AND POOR

In 1929 Sister Teresa began work as a teacher at the Loretto schools at Entally convent, Calcutta. It was not until she had been there for nearly twenty years that God would call her out to do things that would make her name known all over the world.

There were two schools at the Entally convent. At one the girls were mostly orphans or from broken homes; the other, St. Mary's, had pleasant, friendly day girls and boarders from well-off Indian homes. It was at St. Mary's that she taught history and geography.

From her own room, however, she could see hundreds of little red-tiled slum huts crowded together just beyond the convent wall, so different from the beautifully trimmed lawns and colorful flower beds of the convent. Just now, Sister Teresa had nothing to do with the slums. She was busy coaching young nuns for exams and looking after the sick as well as teaching her neat, tidy girls at St. Mary's.

Then, after about five years, she was asked to take over a school for very poor children as well as teaching at St. Mary's, and she had her first experience of "the *real* Calcutta." To reach the school meant a walk through the slums. For the first time she saw mountainous refuse heaps where men, women, and children picked through the garbage for tins or bottles or anything that they could use or sell.

Sister Teresa, still in her early twenties, suddenly felt sick and hurried on to see what her extra school would be like— and the children waited to see what their new teacher was like, too.

Women and children in a Calcutta slum.

14

8

SWEEPER AND HEADMISTRESS

"She's a *white* woman," they muttered to one another—"... don't think we'll like *her!*"

Sister Teresa did not much like the school, either. It was a single long room, which had once been a chapel; it was very dirty and untidy. The fifty or so children stared at her as she rolled up the sleeves of her white robe, found some water and a brush, and began to sweep up the messy room. The children went on gaping. This was sweeper's work, for low-caste people, not for teachers! She smiled at them, and some of the girls came forward shyly to help. Uncertainly, some of the boys found her more water. There was no school that day, but when she went back to the convent the room was tidier and cleaner than anyone could remember.

Next day some of the children tried to look a bit tidier, too. Very quickly the fifty pupils became a hundred, two hundred, almost three hundred. It was *fun* to go to school with *this* teacher! There were two more parts to the school—one had been a stable, and she taught other children in a courtyard.

Soon she began to visit the children in the places where they lived. No wonder they were dirty, hungry, and full of sores! She had no money to give away but she could sometimes help with medicine or a little soap ... and always she gave them love. They had never seen a white woman like this before.

Quickly, they had their own name for her, calling out when they saw her.

"Ma!"

"Mother!"

Then, added to all this work, in 1937 she was appointed Headmistress of St. Mary's school in the convent.

9

THE VOICE IN THE TRAIN

The girls at St. Mary's school were delighted when she was made Headmistress, for they greatly loved their gentle white teacher. Indeed, some of these wealthy girls were already going out with her into the slums to work with her as she cared for the sick and old in their rooms and huts.

Teresa would never see her own mother again, but she wrote to her very regularly. "I am sorry not to be with you," she wrote after her appointment, "but be happy because your Agnes is happy ... everyone wishes me well."

Her mother, Drana, wrote gently in a way that made the new Headmistress think very hard. "Dear child," she wrote, "do not forget that you went to India for the sake of the poor!"

Teaching schoolgirls, wealthy ones or poor ones ... was this what she *ought* to be doing? It was nearly ten years after Drana's letter that God gave her his answer. She was sure he did so very clearly, that she heard his voice even though the railway carriage was crowded with Indian people.

"I was traveling to Darjeeling by train," she explained afterward, "when I heard the voice of God. I was sure it was God's voice, and I was certain he was calling me. His message was clear. *I must leave the convent to help the poor by living amongst them....*"

The date was September 10, 1946, and that day has always been kept by those who later worked with Mother Teresa as "Inspiration Day."

10

CLOSING THE CONVENT GATE

If someone told *us* they had heard God speaking to them we would
probably say they had been dreaming. Mother Teresa's friends—
the Mother Superior in the convent, her parish priest, the bishop
himself—did not say that, but they had very long interviews with
her. "You're absolutely certain that God wants you to leave here
and live in the slums?" they asked.

Her answer was always the same. "*Quite* certain. So that I can
serve *the poorest of the poor.*" Then she went on. "And not only
me. He wants other nuns to come and live and work *with* me."

That second part would not happen at once. For the moment
there was only Mother Teresa, as she became known everywhere.
She was given permission, after some months, to leave the
convent, but she would always have to keep the promises she had
made as a nun. She was sent to a country hospital for six months,
because she would need to know more about illness and disease.
She could stay, when she came back, with another group of nuns,
the Little Sisters of the Poor. But just what *else* would she do? That
was not easy to answer.

In her room she spent a long time in prayer. She folded up her
white robe and in its place put on what she would always wear
afterward—a thin white cotton sari with a blue border, the
ordinary dress of Indian women in town or village. Then she went
out of the convent grounds and closed the gate behind her.

This time, unlike her departure from Skopje, there were no
crowds to wave good-bye.

11
MOTI JHEEL

All her life there had been people to tell her what to do, but now Mother Teresa was on her own.

"Oh God," she prayed, "you have taken me out of the place where I was at least of some use! Now guide me in what to do next!"

First, she needed a place to live in, to work from. But the only money she had was five rupees, perhaps 75 cents, which the archbishop had given her; and Calcutta was crowded with refugees. There were no empty huts anywhere.

"Try Moti Jheel," a friend suggested—the sprawling slum district over the convent wall—and there she *did* find a small, dirty hut for five rupees a month rent. She was a good teacher, she told herself; she would start a school!

A friendly man cleared the weeds and dirt from an open space, and Mother Teresa sat down with two children and began to write Bengali letters in the dust. Next day there were more children sitting with her, and then more. "We're going to school!" they shouted, gleefully. Someone gave her a chair, a table, a cupboard—it was a *real* school, with even more children, all in the open air. She washed their bodies and their hair, put ointment on their sores, gave them prizes when they did well—not sweets, but soap.

When she moved into her hut there was suspicion and hostility. Who *was* this woman? Was she spying on them? Trying to convert them? To kidnap their children?

As she lived among them in their poverty, here, too, she became their "*Ma*"—Mother.

A Missionaries of Charity teaching school.

THE WORK

In 1990 there were 'Houses' of Sisters or Brothers throughout the world:

- 20 in India
- 61 in the rest of Asia and the East
- 45 in Africa
- 39 in the United States and Canada
- 12 in Australia and Papua New Guinea
- 63 in Central and South America
- 50 in Europe

Types of work vary from one country to another but include

- schools in the slums
- homes for dying people who are destitute
- children's homes
- welfare clinics
- traveling clinics
- dispensaries
- help for drug addicts
- help for AIDS sufferers
- soup kitchens
- soup runs for the homeless sleeping out and sleeping rough
- family visiting
- hospital visiting
- prison visiting

Daily tasks: giving bread to the poor, tending the sick, feeding the children.

12
SO MUCH TO DO!

From a distance, she did not look very different from the Indian women in the narrow lanes and bazaars. She was about the same height, rather thin, wearing the same clothes as they did, though her white sari, washed every day, looked cleaner than their drab faded red or blue ones. But her face was different—not its color, for she had long been tanned by the hot climate—but she looked so gentle, so unworried, with bright, kind eyes.

She no longer had to ask God what to do—there was so much to be done that she now had to ask God for strength to do it, and wisdom to choose the right things. Certainly she could not do it all on her own. She needed *help*—money, food, medicines, and people to share the work with her. Especially people ... people who loved God.

Girls from St. Mary's school, where she had been Headmistress, came in their lovely Indian clothes, down the dirty lanes. They knelt beside their beloved Mother in dark huts or narrow alleyways to care for helpless old men or women and give them a little food; to pick up frightened children with fever, or with bony bodies, and cuddle them against their bright saris as they shivered or cried.

It was from girls like these that Mother Teresa's first full-time helper would come, the first of the new Missionaries of Charity.

13

A PLACE OF HER OWN

Very soon Mother Teresa's hut in Moti Jheel was too small and she told Father Henri, her parish priest at St. Teresa's church, how it was crowded by people with children running in and out. She had no time, no private place to read her Bible, listen to God, or pray.

Father Henri was visiting in his parish when God sent the answer. He was with Michael Gomes, a member of his church, and they were talking about her problem when Gomes's eight-year-old daughter broke in. "Daddy, now your brothers have gone away, there's only you and me! Mother Teresa could have a room upstairs ... she could have *all* the upstairs!"

And so Mother Teresa moved into a place of her own, though she was not by herself for long. One day, while she was praying, there was a knock at the door. Outside stood a Catholic girl from St. Mary's school, beautifully dressed, wearing lovely jewelry.

"Subhasini Das!" cried Mother, delighted. "Come in!"

"Thank you, Mother. But I want to *stay*! I've come to say I want to join you in your work for the poor."

Deeply moved, but anxious that Subhasini should not be acting on the spur of the moment, she sent her away "to think about it." When the girl came back a few days later she was very plainly dressed, without jewelry. This time there was no doubt she had come to stay.

Other girls followed her. By May there were three, by November five, and by the end of 1949 there were seven "Sisters" in Mother Teresa's "community."

CALCUTTA

Calcutta has long been an important Indian city. When Britain was ruling India as part of the British Empire, it was the main center of government, though that was moved to New Delhi in the 1920s.

It has always been a very large city, too, but the population grew enormously during the war with East Pakistan (now Bangladesh), when millions of Hindu refugees fled into India, mainly through Calcutta. Almost all of them were village people who had had to leave everything behind them. They added greatly to the problems of homelessness and poverty, which were already immense in Calcutta.

The government could not provide work, food, or homes for the people of Calcutta. There were immense slum areas and thousands of people made their "homes" on the pavement or on any open space they could find. "Home" meant no more than a few pieces of wood with a bit of sacking thrown over them for shelter. Many hundreds of homeless people simply lay down on steps, station platforms, house doorways, or pavements to sleep, and begged for something to buy food during the day.

Calcutta is now one of the largest cities in the world, with a population of over 9 million people. Many of them are still without work, money, or proper homes.

(Below) Sacred cows roam through the back streets. Most Indians would rather starve than kill one for food. (Right) Street scenes.

14
"GOD KNOWS WHAT WE NEED"

God had sent her into the city to serve the poor—but there were all sorts of poor people. He had sent her to serve the poorest of all—but who were they? Many people would have worked out a program of things to be done ... talked it all out with those who were at work already ... made a list of what was most important or most urgent. But not Mother Teresa. She had no list, no organization. She believed God knew what he wanted done, and he would show her.

When she or her young, eager workers saw something that needed doing they tried to do it. But, even doing that much, they needed a great many things. They would kneel down to clean and bandage people where they lay on the path, for there was nowhere else to take them. They gave them medicine in the narrow lanes between the squalid huts, for there was no clinic or dispensary.

"God knows what we need," said Mother Teresa when they told her all that happened, in their rooms upstairs in the evening.

She was not surprised when the local church, St. Teresa's, cleared the ground at the side of the church, put up a shelter with a thatched roof—and so provided Mother Teresa's first dispensary. It was crowded from the very first day.

The young Sisters went from door to door, or from shop to shop, asking for food, money, even medicine—and there was never too much but always just enough to go around.

But soon they were going to need bigger things than that!

15
NO PLACE TO DIE

Every night scores of people lie on the Calcutta pavements, against the walls or in doorways, covered only with the thin sheet they wrap round them during the day. It was so when Mother Teresa began her work, too. Some are ill, some are old; all of them are homeless. Mother Teresa found a man like this dying by the hospital wall.* He was dead by the time she came back to him.

That night as she talked with her young Sisters in Michael Gomes's house, she was dreadfully distressed. "It is bad that people have nowhere to *live*," she said. "But if they have no place to *die*, that is terrible! I must find a place somewhere!"

It proved to be even more difficult than she thought. People knew about homes for old people, for abandoned children, even sufferers from leprosy ... but a place to *die* in!

Then, at last, an important official on the City Council said he thought it was a disgrace to the city that people should just die on the street and he had the very place she needed. Mother Teresa was astonished. On the riverside, at Kalighat, was Calcutta's most famous Hindu temple, always thronged with pilgrims to the goddess Kali. Just below its silvery roof and walls was a long, low, empty building.

"The pilgrims would never allow us here!" she said.

But very soon afterward they *were* there. The notice board outside said:

It meant "The Place of the Pure Heart."

* See chapter 1 for the story.

27

16
"THE PLACE OF THE PURE HEART"

"The pure in heart will see God," Jesus had promised, and that was what Mother Teresa longed for—that by serving God in this way she and her Sisters would help people to see what God was like, full of love and pity.

She was right to be uneasy, for there *were* objectors. Angry young Hindu men threw stones and bricks at the building, and at her. They complained that these women were trying to convert dying Hindus to Christianity. The place must be closed down. It was an insult to Kali, the goddess of the temple.

The Police Commissioner met them, and made a promise. "I *will* close it down," he agreed, and the angry Hindu youths were delighted. Then he went on. "But I will only do so when you bring your mothers and your sisters to do what these Christian women are doing!"

They went away, still angry, but no one came to help. Nirmal Hriday stayed open—always open, for its doors were never closed by day or night.

There are two wards, for men and women, but this is not a hospital. The wards are full but these people will never get better. The Sisters—and there are volunteer helpers, too—go quietly from one low bed to another, giving medicine, comforting people, holding them when they are in pain. These big rooms are perhaps more quiet and peaceful than anywhere else in the great noisy city. People die almost every day, but they die quietly, among those who care about them, perhaps almost for the first time in their lives.

No one else had done anything quite like this, and it was because of this loving work that Mother Teresa's name began to be known all over India, and then around the world.

A ward in Mother Teresa's home for the destitute and the dying.

28

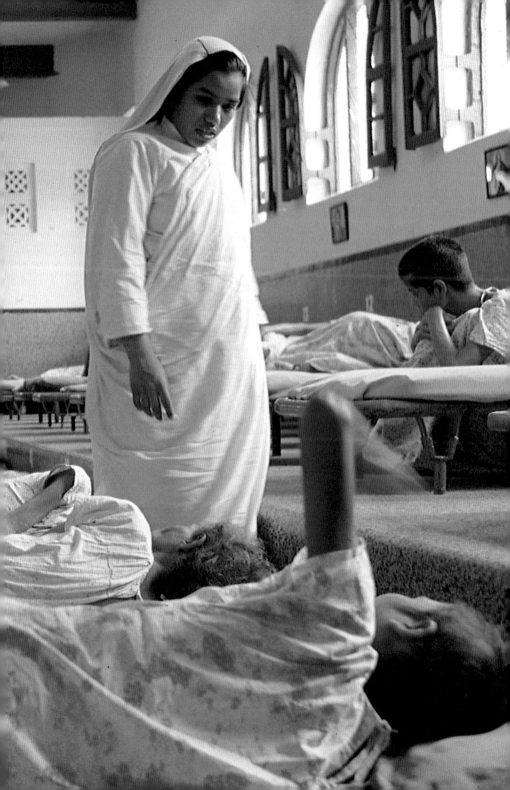

17

THE MISSIONARIES OF CHARITY

Mother Teresa herself had to get permission from her church authorities in Rome to leave the convent and work among the poor of Calcutta. Young women quickly came to share in the work, starting with Subhasini Das, who soon became a nun herself. So Mother Teresa asked permission to start a new "Order" of nuns to do the work she was doing. A year or more passed before the church authorities agreed, and by that time she had a dozen eager young women living with her in Michael Gomes's upstairs rooms. The space was far too small, and as more women came to join the new Order, they prayed every day that God would find them something bigger.

"And, of course, he did!" reported Mother Teresa in her letters home. A big house was sold to them cheaply in the city on Lower Circular Road. It became, and still remains, the headquarters of the new Missionaries of Charity.

Mother Teresa, as head of the Order, drew up the rules.

"Get up at 4:00 in the morning ... prayer until 6:30 ... then breakfast." Of course there was cleaning, and washing, and other household chores to be done. At 7:30 in the morning they went out to schools, clinics, leprosy centers, the home for the dying, or on the streets and in the slums until 7:30 in the evening, with a break for lunch at midday. After supper they talked about what was happening and then, again, prayers ... and bed.

No one had much difficulty in going to sleep!

18

THE BAREFOOT GODDESS

A terrified bull tore down the alleyway between the huts, scattering people as they scrambled to their feet. How it had gotten into the lane no one knew. Children screamed beyond the woman in the white sari, and she got quickly to her feet and stood in front of them. In front of the raging bull, too. She spread her arms wide, standing in its path, and the animal came to a sudden halt, skidding toward her. Then it slowly turned around and ambled back the way it had come.

Mother Teresa was often in danger, though not often from animals (of course, there was always the chance of being bitten by a rabid dog and getting rabies). She had more chance of catching some infection from the sick people she dealt with, or even from the polluted air.

Like any Indian woman she walked barefoot everywhere, to the horror of Europeans who saw her.

There were other dangers, too. Fanatical priests from the temple wanted to murder her. And the equally fanatical young men who worshiped the goddess Kali in the temple still threw stones. A senior police officer was at the riverside one day when they did so, and he called them over, angrily.

"We Hindus think the goddess Kali is there in that temple," he said. "But I tell you this! This Christian woman who walks barefooted through our slums and serves our people ... *she* is the real goddess, and she comes to us with love! Leave her alone!"

31

19
REFUGEES

Mother Teresa had very strict rules in her Mother House, which was now getting full with the growing number of Sisters working with her: rules about prayer and worship; about looking after themselves properly; about eating properly, too—they worked hard and they needed good meals, even if the food was very simple. She had one rule that was always kept. "We never give anything to eat at the Mother House door ... we will never stop people coming, but we provide food in other places and they must be sent there."

But it happened that Mother herself went to the door when a man begged for food. He told her about himself and Mother went into the kitchen, picked up a full plate, and gave it to him. "Eat it at once," she ordered.

The Sister in the kitchen was shocked. "We *never* do that, Mother! And it was Sister Mary's dinner!"

"Then," said Mother Teresa, "Sister Mary must go hungry for once. He has had nothing at all. He is a refugee!"

She had seen them arriving from the war area—filling the railway carriages, holding on outside, clutching the carriage roofs, dropping to the platform as the trains slowed down. In the stations they lay on the platforms, in the entrance halls, on the pavements outside, in the toilets and the refreshment rooms ... thousands of hungry, homeless people with no friends and no future.

One dinner at the Mother House door would not help very much! She sent some of the Sisters with medicine, bandages, food; then she found a space opposite the station and opened a clinic and a feeding center.

"Not much?" she said to a critical passerby. "No! But God only expects us to do what we can. We can do more if *you* help."

20
ALL AROUND THE WORLD

Letters came from different parts of India and from other countries, asking Mother Teresa to send some of her Sisters to begin the same caring work for the poor in other places. But she had always had to say "No." The church authorities had said that she must prove that God had called her and her Sisters to this work for ten years in Calcutta itself. But as soon as the ten years were over she began to move out. First in India, to cities like Bombay and Delhi, and then to other countries in South America and Asia.

Her most exciting invitation was from the Pope himself, sending her a round-trip air ticket to Rome. She found in that great city many desperately poor people, some so sick that the Sisters who began work there had to go to the markets begging for food for them.

She herself, now, was always on the move. The doctor said she was overtired and needed to rest in bed. She tore up his prescription and set off on the plane for South America. She had a broken arm—but it did not prevent her flying to Australia with some Sisters to work with the Aboriginal people. In London she saw men and women living in cardboard boxes ... in Jordan the Palestinian refugees were shivering through the winter, hungry and living in desert skin tents. Something must be done for them all.

Now that they were free to be on the move, the Sisters—Indian, European, American, and others—began to be seen and known everywhere, "working for the poor for Jesus' sake," as they all put it.

21
"LET THE LITTLE CHILDREN COME"

The picture in the Calcutta paper showed Mother Teresa cuddling a tiny baby, only a few days old. The caption under the photo said there were four other babies. All five of them had been left in the Sisters' hospital when their mothers walked out. "*I* don't want it," each of the mothers had said. "Find someone who does!"

Mother Teresa wanted them. When the hospital asked if she would take one of them, she said she would take all five!

"But we're *always* having babies left ... a hundred or more every year!"

"Very well," said Mother Teresa, "we will take them all. That is why we opened Shishu Bhavan."

This drab, two-story building with an open courtyard is her feeding center for the hungriest of Calcutta's poor people. It is

always filled with people waiting for their bowls of hot food. But the really important work of Shishu Bhavan is done for the children. They are brought in every day, by the police or by ordinary people. "I found it in the gutter ... on my doorstep ... in a garbage bin ... on the pavement." Sometimes young girls come with their own new babies and leave them at the Sisters' feet.

Many of them die; some are permanently handicapped. But many of Shishu Bhavan's first children are now grown up, hard at work, happily married, with children of their own they would never give away.

Mother Teresa has always said she is there to serve the poorest of the poor, in the name of Jesus. To many who see her work, that means the children whom nobody wants. If Jesus said, "Let the little children come," Mother Teresa has said the same, year after year.

Children waiting for their food
in Shishu Bhavan.

22
A GIFT OF LOVE

Mother Teresa and her Sisters of Charity have no money of their own; they have to rely on the help they are given all over the world. It comes from all kinds of people, in little gifts or sometimes very large amounts. That was why Mother Teresa was meeting a man representing one of the biggest medical-drug companies in India. Perhaps he wanted to make a big donation. Or give her a regular supply of drugs and medicine.

He gave her something very different. His company—ICI India—was leaving its big office building in the middle of Calcutta. "If you can make use of it, we would like to give it to you for your work," he said.

She could hardly believe that God was being so generous!

"*Prem Daan*, that is what it is," she nodded. "Prem Daan—a Gift of Love!" And so it has been called ever since. Very soon the floors of the big rooms were covered with beds and sick people. This was not a "home for the dying" but "a home for people to get better"—and always there were those who were going out, happy and well, as other sick were brought in. A special part of Prem Daan was set up for the mentally disturbed—and even if they were violent and dangerous, Mother Teresa could be found holding them in her arms, gently quieting them until their violent moods were over.

At Prem Daan and the Home for the Dying in particular, or among the babies at Shishu Bhavan, other workers always assisted the Sisters. Many of them were volunteers. The visitor might well find a local doctor giving six months' service, an American or Australian student scrubbing floors, or a young British nurse caring for the helpless and the sick.

23
BROTHERS AS WELL AS SISTERS

Coconuts provide one of India's most popular and cheapest drinks
but nobody wants the great fibre-covered shells. They are left on
the street, or under the trees where they fall, and add to the huge
garbage piles where the poor scramble to find something for
salvage. But some are left outside the back door of Prem Daan.
And, inside, women earn 25 cents or so a day by stripping the fibre
from the shells and making it into ropes or bags.

"Nothing is worthless," says Mother Teresa, "and nobody is
worthless to God, either."

The Sisters could do a great deal. When Mother Teresa was
going to visit Australia she sent one Sister to the dock area at
Kidderpore on the river at Calcutta. "We should·do something
there!" she said, but gave her no orders about *what* to do. Yet when
Mother came home a few months later there was a school for the
children, a dispensary for the sick and work for the women. It was
what Mother Teresa expected to happen!

Some things were probably better done by men than
women—dealing with drug addicts, or alcoholics, or violent
teenagers on the run, or young criminals. Very soon after her work
began to spread more widely, 'Brothers of Charity' were added to
the 'Sisters of Charity', many of them working, at first,
in the Indian cities or in Vietnam where the Americans
were at war with the Communists.
It was not long before the
Brothers, too, were at work
all over the world.

L E P R O S Y

Leprosy is a disease found almost entirely in tropical countries. Because no one knew how it was caught or passed on, people regarded it as a curse sent by the gods.

It showed itself by colorless areas of flesh and skin that had no feeling. In time it attacked the muscles of hands and feet, so that fingers and toes curled up and, because they, too, had no feeling, hands and feet were often badly burned or cut.

A Norwegian doctor first discovered the "bacillus" that caused the disease and in the years that followed many Christian missionaries provided homes, villages, and hospitals for leprosy sufferers who were still turned away from their families or thrust out of the community or the village.

In the 1940s missionary doctors, mainly working closely with the International Leprosy Mission, were able to use new drugs to cure leprosy. Treatment often took a long time. Fairly soon most of the leprosy

Leprosy sufferers learning new skills at a rehabilitation home.

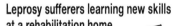

hospitals closed down their longterm wards and started treating people by either visiting hospital clinics or traveling to leprosy clinics.

Leprosy is still greatly feared by most rural Indians, who often do not know that it can now be treated in the same way as any other disease.

You should *never* say "leper." It is regarded as a word that "writes people off" or seems to despise them. It is forbidden in official writing or in the newspapers or the media by the government of India. You should always say "someone with leprosy," "a leprosy sufferer" or "a leprosy patient"—*never* "leper."

Regular surveys of schoolchildren help to prevent the spread of leprosy, and also reduce the stigma attached to the disease.

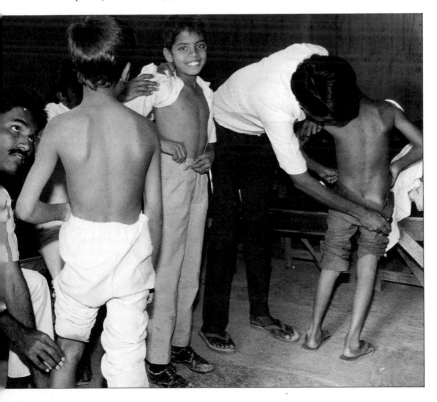

24
POOREST OF ALL THE POOR

Very soon after the Home for the Dying was opened, Mother Teresa came to its open door and found a man lying on the steps. He had not dared to try and come in. She lifted him, carried him inside— he was so thin that he was no burden—and laid him on a bed. It was obvious that he had leprosy.

Leprosy was the world's most terrifying disease. No one knew where it came from or how it was passed on. It was a curse from the gods! Those who contracted it were thrust out of the family or driven out of the village, to end up begging in the streets of a nearby town.

"Never touch anyone with leprosy!" Europeans said it as well as Indians.

"We must do what Jesus did," said Mother Teresa. "We must reach out to them, touch them, and make them welcome!" So, not only at the Home for the Dying but at Prem Daan, in the lines at the food centers, at Shishu Bhavan, and at the dispensaries, people with leprosy were accepted with everyone else. Mother Teresa began a small settlement for them, finding them work to do and helping them to discover that they had a place in life.

By the time her work was becoming established, Christian doctors in India and Africa knew what caused leprosy, that it could not be passed on by touching someone who had it—and that *leprosy could be cured*. Indeed, by that time thousands of leprosy sufferers were being treated like other patients, at clinics and dispensaries, and were free of the disease.

25

THE PLACE OF PEACE

It was a long, hot ride on a crowded train from Calcutta, but Mother Teresa knew that at Shantinagar she would find peace. Indeed, the name itself meant "The Place of Peace." The village was quite new and the buildings looked very different from most Indian villages. The little huts with their tiled roofs, and paths at the front lined with whitened stones, showed that their owners were proud of them. The larger buildings included a dispensary and rooms for storage. As she entered Shantinagar, the villagers came out of their houses and moved gently toward her while children came in a rush, noisy and eager to grasp her hands. The adults bent to touch her feet in the Indian gesture of love and welcome. Someone put a garland of yellow and red and white flowers over her shoulders. There was no place where she was more welcome than Shantinagar.

She had built the village there because the government had given her a big piece of land after her little leprosy settlement in Calcutta was closed down to make room for other building. All the people in the village were leprosy sufferers. The thing that was special about them was that they were all under treatment—the families living together in the little houses, the men and women in their dormitories—and all would be discharged as "symptom-free" after a time of treatment. Shantinagar was not only a "place of peace." It was "a place of hope" for people who had been the outcastes of Indian society. Mother Teresa served the poor—but these to whom she had brought healing as well as hope had been "the poorest of all the poor."

26
"WE DO IT FOR JESUS"

The Pope leaned forward and pinned his own special medal on her sari, near the silver cross. In England the Duke of Edinburgh presented her with a special award. So did the President of the United States. In Oslo, Norway, she received one of the most important awards in the world—the Nobel Peace Prize. And always she said the same kind of thing in reply.

"*I* am nobody ... just the one God chose to do his special work for the poor. Don't remember *me*! Remember the poor!"

Almost seventy years old, she retired as head of the Missionaries of Charity in 1980, after fifty-one years in India, half of them in the service of the poorest of the poor. Her mother had once told her, "Poor people are God's special people." If only the world could see and understand that! She prayed every day that more would do so.

A visitor to the Home for the Dying saw a volunteer washing a man from the street, dirty, and thin as a skeleton. "I wouldn't do that for a million dollars," said the visitor, and turned away quickly.

"Neither do we," responded Mother Teresa. "*We* do it for *love.*"

But not just for love of the poor.

The reason for all those years of service was much more important. If their Lord had been sick, ill, rejected, hungry, dying on the streets of Calcutta they would have served *him*. And Jesus had said that whoever served those in need served him.

Mother Teresa spoke very quietly.

"We do it for Jesus!"

· F · A · C · T · S · H · E · E · T ·
SOME BOOKS

- *Mother Teresa: the Early Years* by Lush Gjergji (Mother Teresa's cousin); English version by David Porter (SPCK, 1986)
- *Mother Teresa: Her People and Her Work* by Desmond Doig (Collins, 1976)
- *Something Beautiful for God* by Malcolm Muggeridge (Collins, 1971)
- *We Do It For Jesus* by E. Le Joly (Darton, Longman & Todd, 1974)

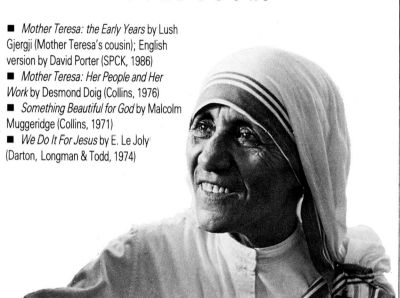

· F · A · C · T · S · H · E · E · T ·
FURTHER INFORMATION

Further information about the co-workers of Mother Teresa may be obtained from:

The Missionaries of Charity
177 Bravington Road
London W9 3AR

The Missionaries of Charity
335 East 145th Street
Bronx
New York 10451